Bruno Johannsson
Come

Eliza Editions
1.1

Bruno Johannsson has a degree in economics from the University of Saarland. He was involved in research and teaching. Poetry accompanied his work from the age of seventeen. In 1976 he published the first edition of this volume in German. He performed readings in Hamburg, Bergedorf, Loccum, Darmstadt, Dortmund, Vienna and Bad Wörishofen. Some of his poems can be found in the annual anthology of the Library of German Poetry in the years 2015, 2016 and 2017.

Bruno Johannsson

Come

Poems

Translation from the German by Hilary Teske

Eliza Editions

Bibliographic information of the German National Library: The German National Library lists this publication in the German National Bibliography; Detailed bibliographic data are available on the Internet at http://dnb.dnb.de.

The work including all its parts is protected by copyright. Any use outside the narrow limits of copyright law without the consent of the publisher is inadmissible and punishable. This applies in particular to reproductions, translations, microfilming, and storage and processing in electronic systems.

Cover Photo Copyright © 2017 Bruno Johannsson

Copyright © 2017 Bruno Johannsson

TWENTYSIX, the Self Publishing House
A cooperation between the Publisher Group Random House
and BoD – Books on Demand

Manufacturing and Publishing: Books on Demand, Norderstedt

ISBN: 978-3-**740744-496**

To my parents
in gratitude

Content
(It may be read as a poem itself.
Please just ignore the page numbers)

Come
The poem of poems

I

Man by the sea,	11
Planted by God,	12
Under the pressure of evil powers,	13
Sinner and saint,	14
Drunk with Thy wine,	16
Amazed,	17
Embarking,	18
Homewards.	19
When do I rise up?	20
How can I serve?	21
A good shepherd I want to be.	23

ASK

In vain?	25
Are we sick?	26
Failed existence?	27
Life?	28
What is playing?	29
Are we rid of God?	30
Does hope remain?	31
Will I find again?	32
Again and again?	33
What should I do?	34
Are we at the end?	36
When at last?	37
When again?	38
Who?	40
Whom does Earth need?	41
Who knows when?	42
Who might hinder it?	43

SAY

End of a winter night.	45
A new day breaks.	46
In pregnant nights one night will be.	48
He will help you.	49
Joyful you go ashore.	50
Breakthrough.	51
Joy in cell 7 777 777.	52
Everything gleams.	54
A breath unites you.	55
Old days shine in.	56
Something new is born.	57
The stadium is already beckoning.	58
One thing is lacking only.	59
Endless in the end.	60
On the high seas Zion will rock.	62
A blaze is sparked.	63
A Man will come.	65
A Prince draws near.	67
From freedom to freedom.	69
The Lord will reign.	70
The very best wine is His blessing divine.	71

PRAY

Beware!	73
Listen to the signals!	74
Turn around!	75
Now!	76
Come near!	77
Forward to life!	78
Roll on!	79
Labor in small things!	80
Men ye must be!	81
Take courage!	83
Feast upon the word!	84
Judge yourself and comfort your fellowman!	85
Sow into this time!	86
Love in life!	87
Brave that!	88
Let your spirit be high!	89
Be calm and see and endure!	90
Never leave!	91
Celebrate the feast!	92

I

Man by the sea

My eyes are built into the sea,
drinking and raining into its expanse.

There is the great yearning
of my heart:
peace and harmony in God.

It embraces all the minor yearnings
of my heart.

It moves me to tears.

My tears roll up my beach
and slide back into the sea.

Planted by God

A gardener plants
a small tree in the earth
and in the ground
he rams a stick
by which it can grow tall
to become a tree.

    god
A   planted me
   man

on Earth
and in my heart
he dug his law
which I can live by

        man
to become a
        god.

Under pressure from evil powers

Sin encompasses me
as the thicket does the glade.

From time to time it advances
and suffocates me into a tiny point.

The spark is not yet extinguished,
although it sometimes smelt like it.

I have to spread the light.
I have to enlarge the glade.
That is the demand.
Otherwise I will grow dim
under pressure from evil powers.

Sinner and saint

Guiltless after so much guilt
my soul.
White after so many stains
my garment.
Why?

Because
Thou suffered,
Thou bled,
Thou atoned
for my sin.

Because
I believed,
I repented,
I struggled
with my sin.

Because
I was baptized,
I was confirmed,
I was strengthened
through Thy grace.

Because
Thou forgivest,
Thou touchest,
Thou fulfillest
with Thy grace.

Drunk with Thy wine

Before you I was kneeling
Asking for Thy power of healing.
Thou hast forgiven me.
Now upright I can stand before Thee.
Drunk with Thy Holy wine
I feel so wonderfully fine.
.

Amazed

What did happen to me?
I have lost a little bit of reality.
My eyes were wet with tears
because of the beautiful sound in my ears.

Who was singing beyond the veil
With tender voices bringing hail
To the Lord, the redeemer of man,
Whom I love as much as I can.

Embarking

Yes.
I reach into the fullness
of heavenly good
and barrels break open
for my delight.

Yes.
I feel the hour
fostering this precious thing
and stoke and care for
the fiery, sacred embers.

Yes.
The vistas are ripe
and have long since parted the clouds
that blocked my access
to the sacred beams so long.

Yes.
My soul is free
and setting off for its final battle.
My eyes are wide
to drink the wine so sweet to quaff.

Homewards!

Where Satan seven walls must climb,
if he wants to lead me in temptation,
where addiction, flight and force
have levelled off to stillness,
where dear animals and tender plants
proclaim my God's wise counsel,
where the sun paints paths for me
and my hour strikes in warning,
where in the worst case
I can be saved by saints.
This is where my home is.

The chaotic traffic must end.

I know now where I am going.

A whole world is my home.

When will I rise up?

When will a leaf fall,
when is it so withered
that it loosens from the twig?

When will I be dead,
tired of the hardship
pervading this life?

When will I rise up
and ascend to the Son,
who redeems me from sin?

How can I serve?

Should the filth of the world
which is served you all day long,
delect you in the evening too,
when you fall tired on your couch
to get sprinkled by the media?

Should I too stir the dirt
you have walked through so often
and which reaches up to your necks?

Should I raise the level even more
so that the swamp takes away your breath
and then closes your eyes
for the rest of time
and the beginning of eternity?

Should the sluggish wave bury your heads
and then spill over to drown your homes and land?
Or do I have to prove to you
that I have bathed in the swamp as well,
smeared myself with dirt
and wallowed in the mire?

So that you say:
"Yes, He knows us.
He has combed the suffering of time
and knows our hardship.

But the thicket did not hold him.
He beat a path to the glade.
So let's listen to His message
and see if it brightens our path, too."
You have a right to proof
and shall have it in due course.
But I won't choose the swamp
to wash you of the mire of time.
I will take pure water
and when it fails add chemicals
to burn away what won't come off.

Nor will I plant trees in your thicket
so that you have no more hope.
I want to be the axe in the forest
to make a path for you to the glade.

I won't give rotgut to the beggar
reaching for my bottle
with dry lips
and with the rest of his strength.
I will let him taste pure juice of grapes,
but carefully so he doesn't choke.

For those assembled for the wedding feast
the best wine of the millennium
is just good enough for their enjoyment.

A good shepherd I want to be

From the depths I want to draw
and water the vast pasture.

I will go to the well
and all my sheep shall follow.
I will lower my buckets into the fullness
and they shall empty themselves
dripping into the trough.

Let the weak, sick and poor come to the front!
I want to refresh you to your hearts' content.
Drink the coolness for your boiling blood,
which caused your hands to do evil deeds!
Pluck the rich pasture I have made for you
and gain strength in marrow and bone!

The day will come
when a King will call you
to share his power.
Yes, a King will rush in
and win victory for you.

ASK

In vain?

People awaken
and fall into life
with no surprise.

People die off
as soon as they're born
having barely lived.

In vain?

Are we sick?

Are we taught
this sickness:
to constantly question,
to permanently complain
and to finally act in vain?

Failed existence?

On one of those eighths,
those August days.

Southern sun:
brooding on a barren egg.

Morning mist:
fog around my brain.

Ape pottering about?
Failed existence?

Life?

Guitar.
Voice from a sorrowful heart.
Crooked roofs on the edge.
Life?

On the edge
there are also wheels vibrating.
Engines are droning,
rolling in long columns.
Life?

What is playing?

Game of shadow and light,
Do you reel from space to naught?
Do you stand rigid and unmoving?
Do you stick close to the ground?

Do you even dance around me in a circle?
Do you roam at random, bound by chaos?
Are you the boldest parody of life?
Should I hate or love you – how?

From the wall the tomb of light
is staring down and down.
Light and shadow untamed
go on romping. On and on.

Are we rid of God?

Who are you
that believes in Him?
Is your mind disturbed?
Haven't you heard
what scientists proclaim?

You can listen to them every day.
"No" they say.
It cannot be
that someone rules
over all the earth
or even the universe.
God isn't dead.
He never lived.
We are rid of Him.
Only out of a few hearts
He still has to disappear.

Are you still
one of those
who refuse
and continue
in this insanity -
He lives?

Does hope remain?

"O, how bleak, brittle and barren is life!"

You think so?
Maybe this time only?

"No. No. No.
Not only this time."

"Yes. Yes. Yes.
This time only."

"Not only. Not only".

Still I have hope.
To me, hope
sends hope.

"Not at all.
Despair
unfolds its wings
flying everywhere."

The night is tired.
The morning nears.
The fear is over.
Despair goes home.

Does hope remain?

Will I ever find again?

Blue, yellow or green?
On which am I keen ?
It is
and was
and will be
time.

Victorious floods are spreading.
Vibrating nerves are sending
weightless
shapeless
joy.

But it scatters in the wind.

Will I ever find again
what
wonder
was and
warm?

Again and again?

When in the desert
suddenly falls rain
and abundant green grass
shoots from the grey grave
to salvage
the unheard of treasure
of manifold life,
people thrill
and are struck
with happiness.

But for one moment only.

Happiness flees,
quivering dies,
treasures sink
grassland fades
into the old grave
of desert.

Again and again?

What should I do?

Should I laugh
loudly like a child?
Yes.
But the echo vanishes.
Speechless I listen to the wind.

Should I sing
cheerfully into the wan night?
Yes.
But the fog chokes me.
My long watch is vain.

Should I build
laboriously my tower?
Yes.
But the sky darkens.
It sends a storm.

Should I pray
fervently through still wires?
Yes.
But a shudder seizes me.
Was it fear blowing through my soul?

Should I weep
big begging tears?
Yes.
But the second one doesn't come.
Feeling lags behind.

Should I love
selflessly till death?
Yes.
And the sluices open.
My hardship is gone.

Are we at the end?

Will humanity
keep on riding
the old carousel
of hate, exploitation and war?

Will old orders dissolve
without new
better ones emerging?

Will it continue to go
downhill with us
to deeper and deeper darkness,
to denser and denser fog?

Is Earth preparing
for the big explosion,
which is to catapult us
into the remoteness of space?

Has the countdown long been running
for us all to ascend to heaven?

Are we at the end?

When at last?

When at last
will flickering flames of war
go out?

When at last
will the trembling quake of Earth
subside?

When at last
will the fat and rich nations
give help?

When at last
will iron gates of prisons
open?

When at last
will the nations
close ranks
for the feast
which only a few
believe in
but yet so many
long for?

When again?

End of war.
Burst of carnage.
A strong wind blows.

Again and again,
anywhere,
for some reason
bulbs burn out.

Where this time?
When with us:
A house is left.
A factory stands still.
A store burns out.
A train derails.
A plane crashes.
A nation falls.
A planet dies?

How many bulbs glow?
Billions around the globe.
Then bulbs couple
and bring new bulbs to light.

Our course is glowing and extinction.
But burning out
can't we evade that fate?

Who was not once in danger
of burning out?
But a friend was there
and we glowed once more.
A father wept
who was prepared to help.

Will we ever know
the secret
of the steady flame?

When will a wind blow
from that sphere divine
over the dross of Earth
and the crusts of men?

When will the ball
jump again
in the eternal whirl
of lasting joy
before shining eyes
of playing children?

Who?

This morning is so full of green
that the red roofs become points,
huts are fading on the slope
nobody can ever disturb.

Who has mixed these colors,
the thousandfold green,
capturing all things today?

Who has sketched in the road,
laid that path in the waves,
so swaying?

Who has caressed this land
that such gently rolling hills
have emerged?

Who has knitted that forest
garlanding the horizon
as if adorning a bride?

Who?
You.

Whom does Earth need?

Alexander or Aristotle?
Caesar or Horace?
Napoleon or Goethe?
Adolf or Einstein?

Who served more?
Whom does Earth need?

Alexander Aristotle?
Caesar Horatius?
Napoleon Goethe?
Adolf Einstein?

Could they save us if they existed?
Who will dissolve the knot for us
which Alexander has smashed in vain?
Whom does Earth need?

Jehovah.
The Lord of Sabaoth,
The Great Emanuel
Jesus Christ.

HE dissolves the knot for us.
HE makes us free.
HE buys us out.

Who knows when?

Nobody knows
when the war will start
which will finally end
the quarrels and battles
of men.

Nobody knows
when the gate will open
which will finally lead
to the kingdom and presence
of God.

Nobody knows?

Someone knows .

Oh, my Father!
Thou knowest.

Who might hinder it?

The time is there.
The day is near.
The bridegroom woos the bride.

Light shadows the feast is casting
on the land.

Daily routine is still groaning
in the woodwork.

But the feast day is approaching.

Who might hinder it?

SAY

End of a winter night

Oh long winter night,
driving all life to flight!
How it held us captive:
the earth so hard
burying all seed.

But now it's gone.
Spring has won
with balmy breath
emerging from buds
touching our cheek.

A new day breaks

Standing in the dark
you tune your senses.
Your eyes pierce the night.
Seeing they cannot see.
Your ears are pricked.
Hearing they cannot hear.
You suck in the black air
and lick the darkness,
to acquire a taste for it at last.

A new space you entered,
tender waves so close.
An inkling comes to you
stealing your sleep
in many a long night.
But your organs,
otherwise so strong,
cannot grasp this sphere
to which you already belong.

Parted fingers foremost
you plunge your arms,
into the dark flood
to seize it.
It gives no hold.

Confess 'I'm seeking'
and the new day breaks
which night can follow no more.

In pregnant nights one night will be

When certain birds are singing
spring is near.
When you awake at night,
because buds are springing,
you remember why:
in pregnant nights
one night there was
in which you leapt
and burst out to day,
shouting wildly
because of lost security.

When certain songs are heard,
Jesus will come.
When you awake at night
because angels chant
you remember why:
In pregnant nights
one night will be
in which you sing
and will be brought to light
smiling sweetly
because of regained security.

He will help you.

When you have fallen,
Jesus says to you:
Stand up!
Be full of hope!
I will help you.

When you go forward,
Jesus says to you:
Go on!
Beware of pride!
I will help you.

Joyful you go ashore

A new shore beckons.
You plunge into the tide.

The new shore changes.
You begin to doubt.

The old shore beckons.
You swim and are disheartened.

The old shore changes.
The last doubt flees.

The new shore shines.
Joyful you go ashore.

Breakthrough

The rouble is rolling.
The streams are flowing.
From inside storms are blowing.

Attention!
The game is starting.
The crust is arching
into the crack.

Booed out,
got rid of at last,
the poisonous guys!

The wedge is forming.
The front gives way.

The signal sounds:
Breakthrough successful!

Joy in cell 7 777 777

Music blows softly past my ear.

It eventually gets caught
in the depths of its tender conch.

Shrill chirping
 is caused by the ear wax,
on which at least a few tones
start to slip and slide.
Others fall silent in fright at such a swamp.

But those which get through
knock on the eardrum.
They are swallowed
and then, as if by a trampoline,
are catapulted
into the huge passages of the inner ear.

On arrival in the deepest cave,
they drip on the stone of the poor soul,
pile up into gleaming stalagmites
and collapse again into a host of small balls,
which roll unchecked into
the brain's farthest recesses.

They bounce against the door of every cell
where there is still no light.
If it opens a crack, they hop in.
In close combat the decision is made -
light or dark.
Some tones fall by the wayside.
 Like sparks they are smothered in the black flood
and expire into ash.

But others overcome and win through.
The situation is barely mastered
when a message is sent up:
Joy in cell number seven
        seven seven seven
            seven
            seven.

Everything gleams

A feel,
finely woven,
spreads out.

Wires sing.
All within reach.
You're amazed.

A thought,
finely woven,
spreads out.

Pillars soar,
fruitfully binding
gravity.

A talk,
finely woven,
spreads out.

Everything gleams
brilliant in the light
at the end.

A breath unites you

Eyes that weep
and words engulf each other.

The heart is full of that good power
which welds together
and calls you masters of times to come.

Late in the night the feast was glowing
and the early morning marveling.

Birds twitter of the night
which you've spent in love so bright.

Old days shine in

Some old days shine in:
Spicy air,
wonderful past.

Is it the sweet breath of childhood
which amazes you?
Flowers and laughter,
frothy hope of then?

Or does a dream
take you back
to the time
when you were not yet begotten
but already so alive?

Something new is born

Gently rolling hills
dance up towards the sun.

The past lives
flowing into the sea of time.

Something new is born
in the swirl at the eye of a needle.

In the white valley
the torrents from green peaks.

The stadium is already beckoning

Twittering of birds and beating of wings.
Even the roaring of squadrons is drowned.
Children are playing in the garden in front of the house.
At the window a tulip is flirting with a crocus.
Is morning still going round in a circle?

Contours are bathing in milky mist,
melting into the eye over floods of tears.
Buds have already swollen up
to fling out the blossom
before the face of the world.
Is the circle already casting spirals?

By the surging sea the city is greening,
and where the wilderness still dwells,
a garden is ready to bloom.
Soft currents are streaming into the lake.
Women are camping on the shore,
where a lion is crying its first tears
because the sweet lamb is sprawling before it.

The stadium is already beckoning,
in which the circle is rotating,
in which the race will end.

One thing is lacking only

Why do pictures hang on walls
and people die of thirst?
Why do some things burst
and others shrink?
Why is there a palace
next to the shacks of the slums?

Is it you, wretch,
who has failed lamentably
and deserves chastisement?
Or you, fatso and powerful swankpot?
Do you want to devour
the one you ought to feed?
Or are you both to blame
for that sweet balance still being denied?

Now come down from your high horse and
you come up out of your grotto.
Treat one another honestly
so that each gets their share!

Is the way too long,
the path too narrow
for all to walk it?
Doesn't Earth provide
what the billions need
to take their turn on it?

Endless in the end

The walls burst quietly.
It is the warm stream.
Walls tremble from within.
Where mortar binds stone to stone,
the future now tears rifts.

Do you know the country that has no trees?
Have you erred through its vast expanses?
Have you ever arched your glance over hilly dunes
and sunk it into the jagged grounds?
Did you ever lie dying
on the sun's blazing breast,
the storm burying you in a coffin?

Now listen to the whispering of this wind,
which gently caresses your nostrils,
and let the clouds comfort you
and protect your timbering.

Hold out your hand
to capture the sweet dew
now falling on your soul,
and when you're finally filled
move forward and water
that nobody is killed.

Bare are the linden trees
but their sap already is rising.
The winds are hatching the spring.
So you too have hope,
for what you have yearned for so long
is rushing down into the valleys now –
the endless melting in the end.

On the high seas Zion will rock

The tears of the deeply moved
will flood the deserts of the earth.
The laughter of the freed
will plumb oceans in oases.

The senile elderly
will cherish youthful dreams.
The stormy youth
will cultivate old love.

Zion will rock
on the high seas
as Jesus once did
so gently in Bethlehem

on the day of the Lord.

The blaze is sparked

Peace wafts down
from the ceiling of clouds
while last storms
still devastate the land.

The whitening flood
has long rolled by,
bringing after it the fire
to burn in people's hearts.

The glittering blaze
Is already sparked,
has brought forth flames
and launched them into hearts.

So let's play like children
in the sand of time,
which has long been joined
to the shore of eternity!

Let's splash in the lake
and leap like the deer
from the dark forest
in the wide and windy meadow!

Let's plunge into the eye
and listen to the mouth.
Let's rub noses
and grasp our hands!

A man will come

It is good when
    the dead bury the dead,
    the weak support the weak,
    the sick nurse the sick
    the cripples drive the cripples
    the deaf teach the deaf
    the blind lead the blind,
    the poor feed the poor.

But a man will come
and many with him
and they are already on the way
and they will be
    holy,
    loving,
    pure,
    hardworking,
    obedient,
    intelligent,
    wise

and will make

>the poor to abound,
>the blind to see,
>the deaf to hear,
>the lame to walk,
>the weak to brim,
>the dead to rise

and

>the living holy,
>the brimming gracious,
>the laughing pure,
>the walking busy,
>the hearing obedient,
>the seeing intelligent.
>the abounding wise.

A Prince draws near

Walnut shells are playing on the lake,
to little troops uniting
dispersing in a dance.

The wise swan knows their playing
and would have been smiling
if his narrow face had room for wrinkles.

Little waves are hopping to the reefs
and continue rolling in the dark.

A fleet is whistling on the border.
A Prince is playing
sounds from that far country
where He once was King.

Dark blue is resting on the hills
which were so cosy in their green.
Houses snuggle in the gorge.
Gates take up their arms before the night.

Noise shatters
on a severe front of poplars
which have now raised as guards,
their tops whispering the fairy tale
that is withheld from children
because parents listen to false channels:
A Prince, a Prince, a Prince
through the night draws near.
The morning sees him King.

From freedom to freedom He will lead us.

He has given us
freedom
to choose
between life and death.

He has given us
charity
to work
for the living and the dead.

Truth
is then promised us
to act,
to wrest life from death.

Freedom
is then given us
to rule
over life and death.

The Lord will reign

When wild animals hum gentle hymns,
and dense jungle opens narrow paths,

When pale swathes of mist vanish in the sun,
and straight paths come into view,

When oases eat into the desert
and arctics melt under hot cities,

When soldiers wave palm branches
and bombers drop balloons for children,

When envy turns to grace
and hatred bathes in the warmth of love,

When all the buds burst at last
and catapult blooms into the day.

When a thousand colors combine
to flood the earth with golden white.

He will reign.

The very best wine is His blessing divine

Towards the end
of the wedding at Cana,
when the guests
were already drunk,
the Son of Man
served to all of them
the very best wine.

What He did in Palestine
so many years ago
on all Earth He will repeat.
He will be the bridegroom so neat
and Zion His beautiful bride.
All the living He will invite
and those who come He will bless
with the very best wine.

PRAY

Beware!

Fear
the dirty mush
that is legally indefinable,
cannot be registered with the police,
is easily tolerated by society,
dressed for a gala,
spreading quite publicly,
turning into a national custom.

Avoid
what is distributed
like tiny sand
in a thousand moments
over all time,
through the whole country,
helping accomplish
the work
nobody recognizes
as a mess.

Listen to the signals!

Someone who does not hear the fanfares
is still sleeping when the feast begins.

Someone who does not see the bow in the rain
cannot measure faithfulness.

Someone who does not lift their head
before the guillotine swishes
will not find the trace in the wind.

Someone who descends into the earth
when heavens are opening
has made the wrong choice.

Turn around!

The ball is rolling.
You know what you should do
and yet you go on playing.

O barbarous time!
How far does it go!
Death it brings to you.

If you don't want to stop
forces will prevail
which make you perish.

So be warned
as your forefathers were
and turn around.

Now!

As
some time or other the beard has gone,
some time or other the train has left,
some time or other the gate is closed,
some time or other the game is ended.

So
now pluck the prophet's beard,
now board the train of His FUTURE,
now enter the holy hall,
now set on "Victory for the King!"

For
then His smile will bless you,
then you will get the connection,
then the light from His throne will shine on you,
then you will win your life.

Come near!

The time is there.
Heaven is close.

O beware
of the sin of old.

Now come near
to a forgiving Lord.

Be of good cheer!
He will save you.

Forward to life!

At last you hear
His steps.

Have you left the world
behind?
Can you feel deeply in your
mind
the Lord?

Can you guess what is in the
air
hovering above your head and so
clear
as the sun?

Forward, my friend,
forward to life!

Roll on!

His commandments
resemble tracks,
traces in the pebbles
to the railroad station,
straight
or gently curved,
always glittering
before the face
of the sun.

We will glide
so securely
into His FUTURE
when our wheels
roll on them.

Labor on small things!

Take care of the pence
and the pounds will take care of themselves.

If you do not face up to the moment
you will cheat yourself of life.

If you do not fill the cell
you will not discover the universe.

If you do not labor on small things,
you will fail on the big ones.

If you do not convert in time,
you will be denied entry
to the Holy City.

Men ye must be

If you howl with the wolves
the wolves will not bite you.
But men will sound you out
and chase you back to the wolves.
Your horrible howling
will not be heard any more by men.
Finally it dies away
when the wolves perish.

If you swim with men
they will not swim away
but if necessary
they will dive to save you.
At any rate no wolf
will stop your flow.
Soon it will merge
into the sea
of victory .

Men ye must be
to live without end.
And those who live endlessly
they are men .

The Father of men
will send His Son
and the Son of Man
will rise again.
Endless is His name.

Take courage!

Whosoever strives
and steadily weaves
the thread of time
O Lord, to them Thou givest
joy in a faltering life.

Whosoever dares
and never complains
in the swirling stream
O Lord, to them thou handest
the glorious winner's crown.

So strive and dare
instead of miserably
trembling in fear.

Feast upon the word!

Hold fast to the holy word!
It will lead you upward.
Grasp it swiftly!
Stroll along to its sound!
Do not repel what profits you!
Turn to the letters of salvation!

The holy word is from God,
and it is so good.
There's the clarity of the stars.
Jump into it.
Romp around
in the element of your soul!

Judge yourself and comfort your neighbor

Fullness as standard for you,
nothing as standard for him!
Then guilt and blame fall on you
and grace and praise uplift him.

Yet doubt does not destroy you
nor does pride dazzle him,
when the Lord's comfort is in you
and His warning voice reaches him.

Sow into this time!

Sow wherever the seed is falling,
fearless and with a cheerful heart!

Nobody should complain:
I got a raw deal,
I was cheated.

Nevertheless, each man to his own
and cast no pearls before swine,
for they do not comprehend
and trample them in the mud.

The words are so precious.
Let us clothe them in silence!

Love in life!

Become strong and brave
clever and wise,
rich and mighty!

Think and plan,
create and set,
build walls for a solid house!

But if it must be:
leave your house,
forget yourself,
lose your life
out of love.

Love in life!
Live in love!
And you will get
love and life.

Brave that!

Do you really love your enemies?
No?
Do you want to love your enemies?
Yes?
You should love them as Jesus did.

They annoy you.
They bully you.
They harm you.
They hit you.
They hate you.

Brave that.
Brave that.
Brave that.
Brave that.
Brave that.

You love them.
Because Jesus loves them
up to His death on the cross.
Because Jesus loves you
even in the anguish of His soul.

His love is true
and endless
and always new.

Let your spirit be high!

Let the world´s past be far
and the Lord´s future nigh!
Put your sorrow aside
and let your spirit be high
on the Day of the Lord.

Be calm and see and endure!

Let us be calm
in view of things
that are to come!

Let us close our eyes
so that we do not err,
and learn to see!

Let us endure
until the great end comes
and the waves subside
before the breeze
from seaside wafting.

Never leave!

Dark night.
Rich garb.

Drunken flood.
Fiery glow.

Harm so far
Nowhere pain.

Two in the boat
on the high wave
to the port.

God, have mercy!
Peace to our soul!
Shield us
in Thy grace!

Let's learn
to be calm
and never leave
the timeless time
of joy!

Celebrate the feast!

Lift up your eyes
and look ahead!
Don't you see the FUTURE
of the Man
promised long ago?

Who wavers and falters,
who still mourns
cloaked in deep black?

Now laugh and dance,
rejoicing in the high time,
as a King woos His bride!

Celebrate feasts
that outshine
the workday
until it completely melts
in Sunday!

Be clad in beautiful garments
so that the world is surprised
in its need
and eye to eye with death
catches sight of life
indeed!

Epilogue

I am very grateful for Hilary Teske who translated these verses from the German with great accuracy. In cases where some freedom was taken in order to have an English text of poetic dimension I as the author agreed with it or even proposed it in communication with Thea Johannsson who was very helpful in all phases of the work. So I thank her also very much.

Hilary Teske, Thea Johannsson and I hope that the English and American speaking readers can enjoy the feelings and thoughts of the author in the sphere of their own language. And I as the author hope that I was to some degree a medium for heavenly inspiration. At least I very often had that feeling. To the degree these feelings where true I thank God as the source of all true and beautiful inspiration.

Bruno Johannsson
November 2017

Be free to express your feelings
evoked by what you have read.
Write them in your diary
and/or communicate them to
https://bruno-johannsson.jimdo.com/kontakt.
There you will be offered the choice
just to communicate with the author
or to get your feelings published
in the readers forum on the website.
In the latter case you are free to use a nickname.